Doc Solon

Occult Calendar

2024

Fr. Aaron Leitch

Doc Solomon's Occult Press

Contents

Preface

Welcome to the seventh edition of *Doc Solomon's Occult Calendar*. This calendar includes feast days for *many* Archangels and Saints, major Egyptian, Roman, and some Greek Deities, as well as many historical and mythological figures of importance to the Western Occult Tradition. This will make finding days proper for invocations and offerings easy. A later section of the booklet provides short descriptions of each Feast, Holy Day, or the figure for whom the day is important, plus an index to help you find each one.

In order to make astrological elections for your rituals easier, I have included the dates upon which the Sun and Moon enter each sign of the zodiac, when any planet goes retrograde or direct, as well as the dates the seven Planets enter and leave the Zodiac signs wherein they have special dignities: ruling, exaltation, fall, and detriment. A spirit's natural time of governance is when its Planet resides in the sign it rules (though exaltation is also powerful), making these periods perfect for magical work with them. We tend to avoid working with them during their fall (when they are weak) or their detriment (similar to retrograde, often bringing out the worst aspects of the planet).

All of this electional information is presented again in quick-reference charts after the calendar section. You will also find several useful charts such as the Planets' essential dignities, the 28 Mansions of the Moon, and the rulership of the Seven Archangels over the hours of the day and night. I hope this will make your magical timing easier to calculate. This document will be updated yearly.

Finally, I am proud to feature another awesome article by a guest contributor: Andreas Erneus. He is an experienced Solomonic practitioner, an expert Talisman crafter, and one of the leading experts on Solomonic manuscripts and history. (He is, along with such luminaries as Joseph H.

Peterson, one of my go-to experts on the Solomonic texts.) His dedicated quest to decipher and correct the Talismans found in such texts as the *Key of Solomon* has been revolutionary to my own practice.

Andreas' historical explorations have resulted in a somewhat controversial theory concerning the history of Solomonic mysticism and its origins in the Byzantine Empire. In *Solomon and the Key*, he introduces us to an entirely different figure named Solomon – one who lived not in ancient Israel, but in tenth century Byzantium, and who founded his own school of occultism. It appears some of the foundational Solomonic texts that later entered Europe are connected to his teachings and students – suggesting the attribution of his work to the Biblical king Solomon was a later retcon. This provides us a unique view into an obscure – yet vastly important – aspect of the history of Western occultism. Enjoy!

Zorge,
Aaron Leitch, 2023

Solomon and the Key

by Andreas Erneus

In recent years we have learned a great deal by studying the ancient texts associated with the name of Solomon, the legendary founder of the legacy we call Solomonic magic. The works of Damaris Gehr, Julien Veronese, Joseph H. Peterson, Jan R. Veenstra, and others have revealed new details about Solomon's personality, his works, and the history of what we can call the European Solomonic Tradition.

Of course, the primary source of information for our conclusions is *Summa Sacre Magice*, a monumental text on magic compiled by the Spanish magician Berengarius Ganellus in 1346. But also important are the texts of the *Magisterium eumantice artis sive scientiae magicalis* (as well as other texts of the manuscript Plut.89 Sup. 38 from Biblioteca Medicea Laurenziana), the oldest texts of *Liber Razielis*, the manuscripts on the four Rings of Solomon, the manuscripts Halle 14 B 36 and Coxe 25.

Since ancient times, the name of the biblical King Solomon, son of David, has been associated with divine magic. Legends about Solomon's power to control demons are characteristic of both Semitic-Christian and Arabic environments. In particular, the legends are reflected in the ancient text, the *Testament of Solomon*, which describes the demons the king summoned as well as their powers and offices.

However, what we now call Solomonic Magic owes its birth to another man; one found in obscure historical records rather than ancient Biblical mythos.

Yes, the founder and namesake of the Solomonic Tradition was a real person, not related to the biblical king. (Henceforth, we shall refer to him as Magister Solomon, to differentiate him from king Solomon.) He lived somewhere in the 10th-11th centuries, presumably in Byzantium, and was very learned. He knew several languages, was skilled in various types of magic (both Jewish and Arabic), and compiled a corpus of books called *Magica*. In his work he often emphasizes the four sacred languages of magic and the traditions associated with them: Hebrew, Arabic (which he calls Chaldean), Greek, and Latin.

Magica was well known until at least the 14th century, but not a single copy of it has come down to us. Although we do know for sure that some parts of this very work (or its teachings) have survived in separate books: such as *Almadel Salomonis, Semaphoras Salomonis, De quattuor annulis, De novem candarii, Liber Samaym*, and others.

Some legends about the biblical King Solomon say he was given a ring by the archangel Michael. It was this magical ring, bearing the famous Seal of Solomon, that granted the king his power over demons. In a similar light (perhaps not coincidentally), the magical text *On the Four Rings of Solomon* says Magister Solomon made four magical rings of his own. These rings of the "elder (or major) art" granted the wearer protection from the fiery breath of demons (a power later found attributed to a ring in the *Goetia*), as well as the power to summon, command, and banish them; as well as a host of talismanic powers such as love, protection, luck, favor from nobles, dispelling of witchcraft, countering poisons, calming storms, and many other miracles that would be familiar to the legends of King Solomon. Other texts say that "Solomon the wisest did nothing without [his ring], but in battle, and in counsel, and in judgment, he always carried it with him."

According to the legends, Magister Solomon eventually bequeathed his four powerful rings to his four closest disciples. One of these disciples was Toz Grecus – who gives his name to the "Toz Graeci" family of Solomonic texts. (There are several such "families" of texts that would eventually give rise to the Key of Solomon the King as we know it. While the Toz Graeci family is not the oldest example, it is very close to the oldest.) For instance: BnF Latin MS 15127: *Toz graeci philosophi nominatissimi expositio super libros Salomonis de secretis secretorum ad Roboam* (Toz, the most famous Greek philosopher, an exposition on the books of Solomon concerning the secrets of secrets to Rehoboam.). Toz also left behind several books that dealt with summoning spirits. Ganell (author of *Summa Sacrae Magicae*) sometimes refers to them, including a book on the offices of spirits.

The closest disciple of Toz was Honorius, who wrote *Liber Iuratus*. This is the main chain of the great magicians who formed the basis of Solomonic magic. Also we have to assume that part of Magister Solomon's texts made their way into the Latin book *Liber Razielis*.

Thus, we have a biblical king unto whom legend attributes great wisdom and magical power, with particular emphasis placed upon a ring of power. And now we know of another – later – magician who united the occult traditions of several different nations into one coherent system, which has come down to us in various forms, undergoing changes along the way. And, once again, we find emphasis placed upon a set of magical rings and their associated seals. It is not surprising these two personalities were conflated in history, leading to many versions of the "*Key of Solomon*" being attributed to the "king of Israel" or "son of David".

Can we say who the author of the *Key of Solomon* was?

Magica describes a very complex (and sometimes incomprehensible) ceremonial practice, where the making of magical artifacts is very, very time-consuming and not accessible to everyone. So, there were various attempts to isolate practical portions from it, or to modernize the system, to simplify it. It is quite possible that the *Lucidarium*, attributed to Peter de Abano, and which is the predecessor of the *Heptameron*, was one such revolutionary attempt. Yet, on the other hand, the *Lucidarium* was created at a time when the first *Key of Solomon* should already have existed.

The text of that *Key* (if we are to judge from the oldest texts) is precisely the key to magic, not a system of magic. *The Key of Solomon* is a description of a simplified and understandable method based on Magister Solomon's principles, with specific instructions for making magical equipment and instruments, most of which are not as difficult to prepare as those originally described by Magister Solomon himself.

Given that there is a legend about a Greek who found Solomon's book and the secret of his magic was revealed to him, and some manuscripts explicitly mention the name Toz, we can assume that the first *Key* may have been composed by a disciple of Magister Solomon named Toz. Besides, as we said, he had his own works on magic, in which he sometimes gave instructions different from Solomon, his teacher, about what he wrote openly himself.

In any case, by the 13th century there was already a known text with the title *The Key of Solomon*. Although the earliest manuscripts we know of are from the 15th century, they do indeed include some things descended from Magister Solomon's original texts.

~ ~ ~ ~ ~ ~ ~

Andreas Erneus is an accomplished scholar of the Western esoteric texts, traditions, and their history – with a particular focus on the Solomonic cycle of manuscripts. He is currently working on a decades-long project to research, decipher, and correct many Solomonic Talismans – with a particular focus upon the Planetary Pentacles described in the *Key of Solomon*. His work has been revolutionary to our current understanding of these venerable old texts.

Key of Symbols

Used in this Calendar

Zodiac

Aries	Taurus	Gemini	Cancer	Leo	Virgo
♈	♉	♊	♋	♌	♍

Libra	Scorpio	Sagittarius	Capricorn	Aquarius	Pisces
♎	♏	♐	♑	♒	♓

Planets

Saturn	Jupiter	Mars	Sol	Venus	Mercury	Luna
♄	♃	♂	☉	♀	☿	☽

Retrograde = ℞

Direct = dir

November 2023

Sunday	Monday	Tuesday	Wednesday	Thursday	Friday	Saturday
			1 -*All Saints* -*Santa Muerte* ☽ in ♋	2	3 -*Saint Martin de Porres*	4 ♄ dir ☽ in ♌
5	6 ☽ in ♍	7	8 -*St Uriel* ♀ in ♎	9 ☽ in ♎	10 ☿ in ♐	11 -*St Martin of Tours* ☽ in ♏
12	13 dark ☽ in ♐	14	15 - *St Albertus Magnus* -*Ennead*	16 ☽ in ♑	17	18 ☽ in ♒
19	20 ☽ in ♓	21	22 ☉ in ♐ ☽ in ♈	23 -*Thanks-giving* -*Sachiel*	24 ♂ exits ♏ ☽ in ♉	25 -*Moses* -*St Catherine*
26 ☽ in ♊	27 full ☽	28	29 ☽ in ♋	30		

December 2023

Sunday	Monday	Tuesday	Wednesday	Thursday	Friday	Saturday
					1 ☿ in ♐ ☽ in ♌	2
3 ☽ in ♍	4 ♀ in ♏	5	6 -St Nicholas ☽ in ♎	7 -Hanukkah begins	8 ☽ in ♏	9
10	11 ☽ in ♐	12 dark ☽	13 ☿ ℞ ☽ in ♑	14	15 ☽ in ♒	16
17 -Solomon -Saturnalia -St. Cassiel ☽ in ♓	18	19 ☽ in ♈	20	21 -Isis -Winter Solstice ☉ in ♑ ☽ in ♉	22	23 ☿ in ♐ ℞
24 ☽ in ♊	25 -Dies Natalis Solis Invicti - Christmas full ☽ in ♋	26	27	28 ☽ in ♌	29 ♀ exits ♏	30 ♃ dir
31 ☽ in ♍						

January 2024

Sunday	Monday	Tuesday	Wednesday	Thursday	Friday	Saturday
	1 -*Mary Mother of God* ☿ dir	2	3 ☽ in ♎	4 ♂ in ♑	5 ☽ in ♏	6 -*Epiphany*
7 ☽ in ♐	8	9	10 ☽ in ♑	11 dark ☽	12 ☽ in ♒	13
14 ☽ in ♓	15	16 ☽ in ♈	17 -*Robert Fludd*	18 ☽ in ♉	19	20 ☽ in ♊ ☉ in ♒
21	22 ☽ in ♋	23	24	25 full ☽ in ♌	26	27 ☽ in ♍
28	29	30 ☽ in ♎	31			

February 2024

Sunday	Monday	Tuesday	Wednesday	Thursday	Friday	Saturday
				1 -Nut -Imbolc -Trithemius ☽ in ♏	2 -Candlemas	3 -St Blaise
4 ☽ in ♐	5 -St Agatha	6 -Horus ☽ in ♑	7	8 -Eliphas Levi ☽ in ♒	9 dark ☽	10 ☽ in ♓
11	12 ☽ in ♈	13 ♂ exits ♑	14 ☽ in ♉	15	16 ☽ in ♊	17 -Giordano Bruno
18 ☉ in ♓	19 ☽ in ♋	20	21 ☽ in ♌	22	23 ☿ in ♓	24 -Johann Weyer full ☽ in ♍
25	26 ☽ in ♎	27	28	29 ☽ in ♏		

March 2024

Sunday	Monday	Tuesday	Wednesday	Thursday	Friday	Saturday
					1 -Feriae Marti -St. Samael	2 ☽ in ♐
3	4 ☽ in ♑	5	6	7 -St Thomas Aquinas ☽ in ♒	8	9 ☽ in ♓ ☿ exits ♓
10 dark ☽	11 ☽ in ♈ ♀ in ♓	12	13 ☽ in ♉	14	15 ☽ in ♊	16
17 ☽ in ♋	18 -Pope Honorius	19 -St Joseph -Vernal Equinox ☽ in ♌ ☉ in ♈	20	21	22 -Nicolas Flamel ☽ in ♍	23
24 -St Gabriel ☽ in ♎	25 full ☽	26 -Cordad Sal	27 ☽ in ♏	28	29 -Good Friday ☽ in ♐	30
31 -Easter -Feast of Luna						

April 2024

Sunday	Monday	Tuesday	Wednesday	Thursday	Friday	Saturday
	1 -*Veneralia* -*St. Anael* ☽ in ♑ ☿ ℞	2	3 ☽ in ♒	4	5 ☽ in ♓ ♀ in ♈	6
7 ☽ in ♈	8 dark ☽	9 ☽ in ♉	10	11 ☽ in ♊	12	13 ☽ in ♋
14	15	16 ☽ in ♌	17	18 ☽ in ♍	19 -*St Expeditus* ☉ in ♉	20
21 ☽ in ♎	22 -*Passover begins*	23 -*St George* ☽ in ♏	24 full ☽	25 ☿ dir	26 ☽ in ♐	27
28 ☽ in ♑	29 ♀ in ♉	30 -*Walpurg.* ☽ in ♒ ♂ in ♈				

May 2024

Sunday	Monday	Tuesday	Wednesday	Thursday	Friday	Saturday
			1 -Beltane ☽ in ♓	2 ☽ in ♓	3	4 ☽ in ♈
5	6 ☽ in ♉	7	8 dark ☽	9 ☽ in ♊	10	11 ☽ in ♋
12	13 ☽ in ♌	14	15 -Mercuralia -St Dymphna ☽ in ♍	16	17	18 ☽ in ♎
19 -St. Dunstan	20 ☽ in ♏ ☉ in ♊	21	22	23 full ☽ in ♐ ♀ exits ♉	24 -Hermes Trismeg..	25 ☽ in ♑ ♃ in ♊
26	27 -Memorial Day (USA) ☽ in ♒	28	29	30 -Corpus Christi ☽ in ♓	31	

June 2024

Sunday	Monday	Tuesday	Wednesday	Thursday	Friday	Saturday
						1 ☽ in ♈
2 -St. Elmo	3 ☽ in ♉ ☿ in ♊	4	5 ☽ in ♊	6 dark ☽	7 ☽ in ♋	8
9 ☽ in ♌ ♂ in ♉	10	11 -Festival of Weeks begins	12 ☽ in ♍	13 -St Anthony	14 ☽ in ♎	15 -St Vitus
16	17 ☽ in ♏ ☿ exits ♊	18	19 -St Blessed Rose ☽ in ♐	20 -Summer Solstice ☉ in ♋	21 -St. Lazarus	22 full ☽ in ♑
23	24 ☽ in ♒	25	26 ☽ in ♓	27	28 ☽ in ♈	29 ♄ ℞
30 ☽ in ♉						

July 2024

Sunday	Monday	Tuesday	Wednesday	Thursday	Friday	Saturday
	1	2 ☽ in ♊	3	4 ☽ in ♋	5 -Anubis dark ☽	6
7 ☽ in ♌	8	9 ☽ in ♍	10	11	12 ☽ in ♎	13 -John Dee -Re (Ra)
14 ☽ in ♏	15	16 -Set	17 ☽ in ♐	18 -Nephthys	19 -Thoth ☽ in ♑	20 -St Margaret ♂ exits ♉
21 full ☽ in ♒	22 ☉ in ♌	23 ☽ in ♓	24	25 -St Christopher ☽ in ♈ ☿ in ♍	26 -Enoch	27 -St Pantaleon ☽ in ♉
28	29 ☽ in ♊	30	31			

August 2024

Sunday	Monday	Tuesday	Wednesday	Thursday	Friday	Saturday
				1 -*Lughn.* *(Lamas)* -*Edward* *Kelley* ☽ in ♋	2	3 ☽ in ♌
4 dark ☽ ♀ in ♍	5 ☽ in ♍ ☿ ℞	6	7	8 ☽ in ♎	9	10 ☽ in ♏
11	12	13 -*Hekate* ☽ in ♐	14 ☿ (℞) exits ♍	15 ☽ in ♑	16	17 ☽ in ♒
18	19 full ☽ in ♓	20	21	22 ☽ in ♈ ☉ in ♍	23	24 ☽ in ♉
25	26 ☽ in ♊	27	28 ☽ in ♋ ☿ dir	29 ♀ in ♎	30 ☽ in ♌	31

September 2024

Sunday	Monday	Tuesday	Wednesday	Thursday	Friday	Saturday
1	2 -Osiris ☽ in ♍	3 dark ☽	4 ☽ in ♎ ♂ in ♋	5	6	7 ☽ in ♏
8	9 ☽ in ♐ ☿ in ♍	10	11	12 ☽ in ♑	13 -Epulum Jovis	14 -Agrippa ☽ in ♒
15	16 ☽ in ♓	17 -Hathor -St Sophia the Martyr	18 full ☽ in ♈	19	20 -St Eustace ☽ in ♉	21
22 -Autumnal Equinox ☽ in ♊ ☉ in ♎ ♀ in ♏	23	24 - Paracelsus ☽ in ♋	25	26 -St Cyprian & St Justina of Antioch ☽ in ♌ ☿ exits ♍	27	28
29 -Michaelmas -Archangels ☽ in ♍	30					

October 2024

Sunday	Monday	Tuesday	Wednesday	Thursday	Friday	Saturday
		1 ☽ in ♎	2 -Holy Guardian Angels dark ☽	3	4 -St Francis ☽ in ♏	5
6	7 -Maat ☽ in ♐	8	9 -Reginald Scot ☽ in ♑	10 ♃ ℞	11 ☽ in ♒	12
13 ☽ in ♓	14	15 ☽ in ♈	16 -Tabernacles begins	17 -Sekhmet full ☽ in ♉ ♀ exits ♏	18	19 ☽ in ♊
20	21 ☽ in ♋	22 ☉ in ♏	23	24 -St Raphael ☽ in ♌	25	26 ☽ in ♍
27	28 -St Jude	29 ☽ in ♎	30	31 -Halloween -Bast		

November 2024

Sunday	Monday	Tuesday	Wednesday	Thursday	Friday	Saturday
					1 -*All Saints* -*Santa Muerte* dark ☽	2
3 -*Saint Martin de Porres* ☽ in ♐ ♂ exits ♋	4	5 ☽ in ♑	6	7 ☽ in ♒	8 -*St Uriel*	9
10 ☽ in ♓	11 -*St Martin of Tours*	12 ☽ in ♈	13 ♄ dir	14 ☽ in ♉	15 - *St Albertus Magnus* -*Ennead* full ☽	16 ☽ in ♊
17	18 ☽ in ♋	19	20 ☽ in ♌	21 ☉ in ♐	22 ☽ in ♍	23
24	25 -*Moses* -*St Catherine* ☽ in ♎ ☿ ℞	26	27	28 -*Thanks-giving* -*Sachiel* ☽ in ♏	29	30 ☽ in ♐

December 2024

Sunday	Monday	Tuesday	Wednesday	Thursday	Friday	Saturday
1 dark ☽	2 ☽ in ♑	3	4	5 ☽ in ♒	6 -*St Nicholas* ♂ ℞	7 ☽ in ♓
8	9 ☽ in ♈	10	11 ☽ in ♉	12	13 ☽ in ♊	14
15 full ☽ in ♋ ☿ dir	16	17 -*Solomon* -*Saturnalia* -*St. Cassiel* ☽ in ♌	18	19	20 ☽ in ♍	21 -*Isis* -*Winter Solstice* ☉ in ♑
22 ☽ in ♎	23	24	25 -*Dies Natalis Solis Invicti* -*Christmas* -*Hanukkah begins* ☽ in ♏	26	27 ☽ in ♐	28
29	30 dark ☽ in ♑	31				

Planetary Quick-Reference

The following charts will allow you to easily find when each Planet enters and exits the signs of its dignities, and when each Planet enters retrograde and returns to direct motion. The cells are shaded for periods when the Planets are in the Signs they rule. (Note the Lunar Dignities have been moved to their own Quick Reference table.)

First Half of 2024

(r) = Ruling Sign. (e) = Exaltation. (f) = Fall.

(dt) = Detriment. (rx) = Retrograde. (dir) = Direct.

Saturn	Jupiter	Mars	Sol	Venus	Merc
Jan 1 already in ♓	Jan 1 already in ♉	Jan 4 in ♑ (e)	Jan 1 already in ♑	Jan 1 already in ♐	Jan 1 already in ♐ - (dir)
June 29 (rx)	May 25 in ♊ (dt)	Feb 13 exits	Jan 20 in ♒ (dt)	Mar 11 in ♓ (e)	Feb 23 in ♓ (dt)
		April 30 in ♈ (r)	Feb 18 in ♓	Apr 5 in ♈ (dt)	Mar 9 exits
		June 9 in ♉ (dt)	Mar 19 in ♈ (e)	Apr 29 in ♉ (r)	Apr 1 (rx)
			Apr 19 in ♉	May 23 exits	Apr 25 (dir)
			May 20 in ♊		Jun 3 in ♊ (r)
			Jun 20 in ♋		Jun 17 exits

Planetary Quick-Reference

Second Half of 2024

(r) = Ruling Sign. (e) = Exaltation. (f) = Fall.

(d) = Detriment. (rx) = Retrograde. (dir) = Direct.

Saturn	Jupiter	Mars	Sol	Venus	Merc
Nov 13 (dir)	Oct 9 (rx)	July 20 exits	July 22 in ♌ (r)	Aug 4 in ♍ (f)	July 25 in ♍ (r)
		Sep 4 in ♋ (f)	Aug 22 in ♍	Aug 29 in ♎ (r)	Aug 5 (rx)
		Nov 3 exits	Sep 22 in ♎ (f)	Sep 22 in ♏ (dt)	Aug 14 exits
		Dec 6 (rx)	Oct 22 in ♏	Oct 17 exits	Aug 28 (dir)
			Nov 21 in ♐		Sep 9 in ♍ (r)
			Dec 21 in ♑		Sep 26 exits
					Nov 25 (rx)
					Dec 15 (dir)

Lunar Quick-Reference

First Half of 2024

(r) = Ruling Sign. (e) = Exaltation. (f) = Fall. (dt) = Detriment.

Jan		Feb		Mar		Apr		May		Jun	
3	♎	1	♏(f)	2	♐	1	♑ (dt)	2	♓	1	♈
5	♏(f)	4	♐	4	♑ (dt)	3	♒	4	♈	3	♉ (e)
7	♐	6	♑ (dt)	7	♒	5	♓	6	♉ (e)	5	♊
10	♑ (dt)	8	♒	9	♓	7	♈	9	♊	7	♋ (r)
12	♒	10	♓	11	♈	9	♉ (e)	11	♋ (r)	9	♌
14	♓	12	♈	13	♉ (e)	11	♊	13	♌	12	♍
16	♈	14	♉ (e)	15	♊	13	♋ (r)	15	♍	14	♎
18	♉ (e)	16	♊	17	♋ (r)	16	♌	18	♎	17	♏(f)
20	♊	19	♋ (r)	19	♌	18	♍	20	♏(f)	19	♐
22	♋ (r)	21	♌	22	♍	21	♎	23	♐	22	♑ (dt)
25	♌	24	♍	24	♎	23	♏(f)	25	♑ (dt)	24	♒
27	♍	26	♎	27	♏(f)	26	♐	27	♒	26	♓
30	♎	29	♏(f)	29	♐	28	♑ (dt)	30	♓	28	♈
						30	♒			30	♉ (e)

Lunar Quick-Reference

Second Half of 2024

(r) = Ruling Sign. (e) = Exaltation. (f) = Fall. (dt) = Detriment.

Jul		Aug		Sep		Oct		Nov		Dec	
2	♊	1	♋ (r)	2	♍	1	♎	3	♐	2	♑ (dt)
4	♋ (r)	3	♌	4	♎	4	♏ (f)	5	♑ (dt)	5	♒
7	♌	5	♍	7	♏ (f)	7	♐	7	♒	7	♓
9	♍	8	♎	9	♐	9	♑ (dt)	10	♓	9	♈
12	♎	10	♏ (f)	12	♑ (dt)	11	♒	12	♈	11	♉ (e)
14	♏ (f)	13	♐	14	♒	13	♓	14	♉ (e)	13	♊
17	♐	15	♑ (dt)	16	♓	15	♈	16	♊	15	♋ (r)
19	♑ (dt)	17	♒	18	♈	17	♉ (e)	18	♋ (r)	17	♌
21	♒	19	♓	20	♉ (e)	19	♊	20	♌	20	♍
23	♓	22	♈	22	♊	21	♋ (r)	22	♍	22	♎
25	♈	24	♉ (e)	24	♋ (r)	24	♌	25	♎	25	♏ (f)
27	♉ (e)	26	♊	26	♌	26	♍	28	♏ (f)	27	♐
29	♊	28	♋ (r)	29	♍	29	♎	30	♐	30	♑ (dt)
		30	♌			31	♏ (f)				

Lunar Mansions

Determine the degree of the Moon in its current Sign, and the following chart will illustrate the Lunar Mansion in which it resides:

Mansion	Name	Entrance	Exit
1	Alnath	1 Aries	12 Aries
2	Allothaim or Albochan	13 Aries	25 Aries
3	Achaomazon or Athoray	26 Aries	8 Taurus
4	Aldebaram	9 Taurus	21 Taurus
5	Alchatay or Albachay	22 Taurus	4 Gemini
6	Alhanna or Alchaya	5 Gemini	17 Gemini
7	Aldimiach or Alarzach	18 Gemini	0 Cancer
8	Alnaza or Anatchtraya	1 Cancer	12 Cancer
9	Archaam or Arcaph	13 Cancer	25 Cancer
10	Algelioche or Albgebh	26 Cancer	8 Leo
11	Azobra or Ardurf	9 Leo	21 Leo
12	Alzarpha or Azarpha	22 Leo	4 Virgo
13	Alhaire	5 Virgo	17 Virgo
14	Achurethor Arimet	18 Virgo	0 Libra
15	Agrapha or Algarpha	1 Libra	12 Libra
16	Azubene or Ahubene	13 Libra	25 Libra
17	Alchil	26 Libra	8 Scorpio
18	Alchas or Altob	9 Scorpio	21 Scorpio
19	Allatha or Achala	22 Scorpio	4 Sagittarius
20	Abnahaya	5 Sagittarius	17 Sagittarius
21	Abeda or Albeldach	16 Sagittarius	0 Capricorn
22	Sadahacha or Zodeboluch	1 Capricorn	12 Capricorn
23	Zabadola or Zobrach	13 Capricorn	25 Capricorn
24	Sadabath or Chadezoad	26 Capricorn	8 Aquarius
25	Sadalbracha or Sadalachia	9 Aquarius	21 Aquarius
26	Alpharg or Phragol Mocaden	22 Aquarius	4 Pisces
27	Alcharya or Alhalgalmoad	5 Pisces	17 Pisces
28	Albotham or Alchalcy	18 Pisces	30 Pisces

Table of Planetary Dignities

This chart contains the rulerships and dignities of the Planets. It is best to work with the Planets when they are in a sign they rule, or in which they are exalted. Fall is weak. Detriment is similar to retrograde, in that it can bring out the worst traits of the Planet.

	Rules	**Exaltation**	**Fall**	**Detriment**
Saturn	Cap, Aquar	Libra	Aries	Canc, Leo
Jupiter	Sag, Pisc	Canc	Cap	Gem, Virg
Mars	Aries, Scorp	Cap	Canc	Libra, Taurus
Sol	Leo	Aries	Libra	Aquarius
Venus	Taurus, Libra	Pisces	Virgo	Scorp, Aries
Mercury	Gemini, Virgo	Virgo	Pisces	Sag, Pisces
Luna	Cancer	Taurus	Scorpio	Capricorn

The 24 Magical Hours

These are the magical names of the 24 hours of the day and night. (Their origins remain a mystery to this day.) Their functions descend from very ancient systems of astrological magick, adopted into European grimoires from Arabic sources (like the *Picatrix*). The intent is to create Talismans or Images on these hours for the listed purposes. (Note this particular system is rarely used, as it was eventually supplanted by the Solomonic Magical Hours.)

Daytime Hours (begins at Sunrise)

	Name	Function
1	Yayn	Destruction of evil voices, binding of tongues.
2	Yanor	Friendship, grace, boons, ambassadors.
3	Nasnia	Hunting, fishing, birth/delivery.
4	Salla	Binding of woodland beasts.
5	Sadedali	Binding and driving beasts, and any other power.
6	Thamur	Freeing captives.
7	Ourer	Peace between kings.
8	Thainé	Sowing wrath and discord.
9	Neron	Travel, and moving safely among thieves.
10	Yayon	Exorcise demons and panic, and to help mistresses.
11	Abai	Menstruation, and binding men and women together.
12	Nathalon	Peace between enemies.

The 24 Magical Hours

Nighttime Hours (begins at Sunset)

	Name	Function
1	Beron	Goetic operations, summoning demons.
2	Barol	Fishing, and for everything that gives birth in water.
3	Thanu	Light or extinguish fires, or for anything you wish.
4	Athor	Destruction of homes, forced relocation of people.
5	Mathon	Seeing the future via dreams, and revealing secrets.
6	Rana	Gardening, farming, plants, fruits, trees, etc.
7	Netos	Expel people from their homes, cause sickness or death.
8	Tafrac	Building of enmity between others.
9	Sassur	Bind tongues, or gain audience with authority figures.
10	Agla	Destroy gossip, bad thoughts, and false rumors against you.
11	Cäerra	Binding or capture of birds.
12	Salam	Fortune telling, revealing fugitives and criminals.

The Archangel who governs each hour will differ depending on the day of the week you are working. See the following tables to find which Archangels rule each hour of each day of the week:

The Archangels Ruling the Hours

Daytime Hours (begins at Sunrise)

	Sunday	Monday	Tuesday	Wednesday	Thursday	Friday	Saturday
1	Michael	Gabriel	Samael	Raphel	Sachiel	Anael	Cassiel
2	Anael	Cassiel	Michael	Gabriel	Samael	Raphael	Sachiel
3	Raphael	Sachiel	Anael	Cassiel	Michael	Gabriel	Samael
4	Gabriel	Samael	Raphael	Sachiel	Anael	Cassiel	Michael
5	Cassiel	Michael	Gabriel	Samael	Raphael	Sachiel	Anael
6	Sachiel	Anael	Cassiel	Michael	Gabriel	Samael	Raphael
7	Samael	Raphael	Sachiel	Anael	Cassiel	Michael	Gabriel
8	Michael	Gabriel	Samael	Raphael	Sachiel	Anael	Cassiel
9	Anael	Cassiel	Michael	Gabriel	Samael	Raphael	Sachiel
10	Raphael	Sachiel	Anael	Cassiel	Michael	Gabriel	Samael
11	Gabriel	Samael	Raphael	Sachiel	Anael	Cassiel	Michael
12	Cassiel	Michael	Gabriel	Samael	Raphael	Sachiel	Anael

Nighttime Hours (begins at Sunset)

	Sunday	Monday	Tuesday	Wednesday	Thursday	Friday	Saturday
1	Sachiel	Anael	Cassiel	Michael	Gabriel	Samael	Raphael
2	Samael	Raphael	Sachiel	Anael	Cassiel	Michael	Gabriel
3	Michael	Gabriel	Samael	Raphael	Sachiel	Anael	Cassiel
4	Anael	Cassiel	Michael	Gabriel	Samael	Raphael	Sachiel
5	Raphael	Sachiel	Anael	Cassiel	Michael	Gabriel	Samael
6	Gabriel	Samael	Raphael	Sachiel	Anael	Cassiel	Michael
7	Cassiel	Michael	Gabriel	Samael	Raphael	Sachiel	Anael
8	Sachiel	Anael	Cassiel	Michael	Gabriel	Samael	Raphael
9	Samael	Raphael	Sachiel	Anael	Cassiel	Michael	Gabriel
10	Michael	Gabriel	Samael	Raphael	Sachiel	Anael	Cassiel
11	Anael	Cassiel	Michael	Gabriel	Samael	Raphael	Sachiel
12	Raphael	Sachiel	Anael	Cassiel	Michael	Gabriel	Samael

Feasts and Holy Days

Fixed Holy Days

Agrippa born: September 15

Beltane (Mayday): May 1

Christmas: December 25

Candlemas: February 2

Dies Natalis Solis Invicti: December 25

Edward Kelley born: August 1

Eliphas Levi born: February 8

Epiphany: January 6

Epulum Jovis: September 13

Feast/Festival of -

      All Hallows: October 31

      All Saints (All Saints Day): November 1

      Anubis: July 5

      Archangels: September 29

      Bast: October 31

      Cordad Sal (Zoroaster's birth): March 26

      Ennead in the House of Ra: November 15

      Epiphany (Three Kings Day): January 6

      Enoch: July 26

      Hathor: September 17

      Hekate: August 13

      Hermes Trismegistus: May 24

      Holy Guardian Angels: October 2

      Horus: February 26

Isis: December 17

Jupiter: September 13

Maat: October 7

Mars: March 1

Mary, Holy Mother of God: January 1

Mercury: May 15

Moses: November 25

Nephthys: July 18

Nut: February 1

Osiris: September 2

Re (Ra): July 13

Santa Muerte: November 1

Saturn: December 17

Sekhmet: October 17

Set: July 16

Sol: December 25

Solomon: December 17

St. Agatha: February 5

St. Albert the Great (Albertus Magnus): November 15

St. Anael: April 1

St. Anthony: June 13

St. Barbara: December 4

St. Blaise: February 3

St. Blessed Rose: June 19

St. Brigid: February 1

St. Cassiel: December 17

St. Catherine of Alexandria: November 25

St. Christopher: July 25

St. Cyprian (of Antioch): September 26

St. Dunstan: May 19

St. Dymphnia: May 15

St. Elmo: June 2

St. Eustace: September 20

St. Expeditus: April 19

St. Francis: October 4

St. Gabriel: March 24

St. George: April 23

St. Joseph: March 19

St. Jude: October 28

St. Justina (of Antioch): September 26

St. Lazarus: June 21

St. Margaret the Virgin: July 20

St. Martin de Porres: November 3

St. Martin of Tours: November 11

St. Michael: September 29

St. Muerte: November 1

St. Nicholas: December 6

St. Pataleon: July 27

St. Raphael: October 24

St. Samael: March 1

St. Sophia the Martyr: September 17

St. Thomas Aquinas: March 7

St. Uriel (Auriel): November 8

St. Vitus: June 15

Thoth: July 19

Venus: April 1

Feriae Marti: March 1

Giordano Bruno passes: February 17

Halloween: October 31

Hekatesia: August 13

Imbolc: February 1

Johann Weyer passes: February 24

John Dee born: July 13

Lughnasadh (Lammas): August 1

Mercuralia: May 15

Michaelmas: September 29

Nicolas Flamel passes: March 22

Paracelsus passes: September 24

Pope Honorius III passes: March 18

Reginald Scot (Scott) passes: October 9

Robert Fludd born: January 17

Samhain: October 31

Saturnalia: December 17

Trithemius born: February 1

Veneralia: April 1

Walpurgisnacht: April 30

Movable Holy Days 2024

Autumnal Equinox (*Mabon*): September 22

Corpus Christi: May 30

Easter: March 31

Feast of Sachiel (Zadkiel): November 28

Festival of Weeks (*Shavuot*) begins: June 11

Good Friday: March 29

Hanukkah begins: December 25

Memorial Day (USA): May 27

Passover begins: April 22

Summer Solstice (*Litha*): June 20

Tabernacles (*Sukkot*): October 16

Thanksgiving: November 28

Vernal (Spring) Equinox: March 19

Winter Solstice (*Yule*): December 21

January 2024

Jan 1 – Feast of Mary, Holy Mother of God. Also called the Feast of the Solemnity of Holy Mother Mary. Mary was the mother of Jesus, and has been equated with Sophia, the Queen of Heaven, the Shekhina, Aima Elohim, and the Soul of the World.

Jan 6 – Epiphany (Three Kings Day): The first day *after* the Twelve Days of Christmas (Dec 25 – Jan 5). In Western tradition, it commemorates the birth of Jesus and the visit of the Three Magi to the manger. In Eastern tradition, it instead commemorates the baptism of Jesus. During the Epiphany mass, substances such as water, incense, and chalk are consecrated for use in protecting the home. This holy day is mentioned in *The Sixth and Seventh Books of Moses* (see Joseph Peterson's edition).

Jan 17 – Robert Fludd born: Robert Fludd (January 17, 1574 – September 8, 1637), also known as Robertus de Fluctibus , was a Paracelsian physician, scientist, astrologer, mathematician, Qabalist, occultist, and Rosicrucian philosopher.

February 2024

Feb 1 – Imbolc (Feast of St. Brigid): Midpoint between winter solstice and spring equinox. Originally a Celtic seasonal festival, associated with Brigid (later, St. Brigid) the Goddess of Ireland. Imbolc, in modern Neopaganism celebrates the Sun as a growing child, and the first stirrings of spring. Traditionally a time for initiation.

- Feast of Nut: Celebrates the Sky Goddess, wife of Re, lover of Geb, and Mother of the five powerful Gods Osiris, Isis, Set, Nephthys, and Horus the Elder. She is one of the nine principal Egyptian Deities (the *Ennead*).

- Trithemius born: Iohannes Trithemius (b. February 1, 1467) was an abbot, an author, a cryptographer, and an occultist. His most famous works are possibly the *Steganographia* and *De Septem Secundeis id est Intelligentiis* His students included such men as Agrippa and Paracelcus.

Feb 2 – Candlemas: Christian observance of the presentation of a young Jesus to the Temple. A mass is held on this night, during which candles are blessed and sent home to be burned throughout the year. Has obvious relationship to early-spring celebrations like Imbolc.

Feb 3 – Feast of St. Blaise: Celebrates the Patron Saint of wool-combers. The earliest reference to him mentions invoking him to aid treatment of objects stuck in the throat. (As he was a physician in life, he was likely invoked for many healing purposes. It was also said that he healed animals who came to him for help.)

Feb 5 – Feast of St. Agatha: Celebrates the Patron Saint of breast cancer patients, wet nurses, victims of sexual-assault, -abuse, and -slavery. She also protects the home against fire, earthquakes, and volcanic eruptions. (She is also the Patron of bell-makers, because fire alarms use bells.)

Feb 8 – Eliphas Levi born: Eliphas Levi (February 8, 1810 – May 31, 1875) was an influential French author and occultist. He serves as a bridge between the older grimoiric traditions and the later masonic-style lodge systems of magick such as the Golden Dawn. His material is Solomonic, though also influenced heavily by alchemy and Christian Qabalah, and it would become foundational to the philosophies of late 19th Century occultists like Mathers, Westcott, Kingsford, Blavatski, Crowley, etc.

Feb 17 – Giordano Bruno passes: Born Filipo Burno (1548 – February 17, 1600) was a Dominican friar, philosopher, mathematician, poet, astronomer, astrologer, Neoplatonist, and Hermeticist. He is especially famous for his cosmological theories (such as the stars being distant suns, and the universe being infinite), heretical views, and writings on the Art of Memory. He was burned at the stake for heresy on this day.

Feb 24 – Johann Weyer passes: Johann Weyer (1515 – February 24, 1588) was a physician, occultist, and demonologist – most famous for his *Pseudomonarchia Daemonum* (The False Kingdom of the Demons), which had an influence on grimoires such as the *Goetia*. And for his *De Praestigiis Daemonum et Incantationibus ac Venificiis* (On the Illusions of the Demons and on Spells and Poisons). He was a student of Agrippa.

Feb 26 – Feast of Horus: Celebrates the son of Isis and Osiris. A Solar God of war, similar in many ways to the later Archangel Michael. Egyptian mythos records that Horus grew to manhood, defeated Set (the murderer of his father) in open combat, and ascended the Throne. From then on, every Pharaoh was considered an incarnation of Horus himself. One of the nine principal Egyptian Deities (the *Ennead*).

March 2024

Mar 1 – Feriae Marti (Feast of Mars): *Feriae Marti* literally translates as "Holy Day of Mars." This day was considered the birthday of the God Mars, and the beginning of the season of warfare for the year. (It is also near the time when the Sun will enter Aries – which is ruled by Mars.) This is a good day to honor Samael and other Angels of Mars.

  – Feast of St. Samael: Samael is the Archangel of Mars and Tuesday – prince of the fifth heaven (called Machon), lord of war and pestilence, and angel of death and destruction. His name means "Poison of God." He is prince of the Choir of Seraphim.

  He also governs the Sephirah Gevurah (Divine Severity). He is the *Sathan* (Adversary) who accuses man of their wrongdoings in the Divine Court. (Samael should not be confused with the modern Christian concept of the Devil. Samael is not the source of all evil, nor did he ever wage war upon the Throne of God.)

  Samael was at one point regarded as the Patron Angel of Rome. More recent tradition has given him the name Khamael (Camael, Camuel, etc) – the result of mistranslating a Hebrew *Samekh* (S) as a *Kaph* (Kh). In this form he is regarded primarily as the Angel of War and Divine Severity.

Mar 7 – Feast of St. Thomas Aquinas: An extremely influential theologian and philosopher. His feast day since 1969 has been January 28, but it was originally the day of his passing: March 7, 1274. He is the patron of academics, scholars, apologists, philosophers, book sellers, publishers, learning, students, chastity, and pencil makers. Invoked against storms and lightning.

March 17 – Feast of St. Patrick: Celebrates the Patron St. of Ireland.

- **Feast of St. Gertrude:** Celebrates the Saint of Cats, and those who love cats.

Mar 18 – Pope Honorius III passes: This pope passed on March 18, 1227. He is the purported author of the *Grimoire of Pope Honorius*, though there is little evidence to support the claim.

Mar 19 – Feast of St. Joseph: Celebrates Joseph, the father of Jesus. Conjure tradition uses spells involving St. Joseph to help sell one's home, and to help in finding employment.

Mar 19 – Vernal (Spring) Equinox: Also Ostara. The day and night are equal lengths on this day, each one exactly twelve clock-hours long. The official first day of spring. Ostara, in modern Neopaganism, celebrates the overthrow of the "Lord of the Waning Sun" (who presided over winter) and the ascension of the "Lord of the Waxing Sun" (who will preside over summer).

Mar 22 – Nicolas Flamel passes: Nicolas Flamel (1340 – March 22, 1418) was a scribe and manuscript-seller, who developed a reputation as an alchemist after his passing. Legends appeared in the 17th century in which Flamel had discovered the Philosopher's Stone and gained immortality. He has since become a heroic figure in alchemical lore.

Mar 24 – Feast of St. Gabriel: St. Gabriel is the Angel of the Moon and Monday, as well as the first heaven called Shamaim. His name means "Strength of God" and he is prince of the Choir of Kherubim. He is second only to Michael in the divine hierarchy, sitting at the left-hand of God. He is one of the Four (along with Michael, Raphael, and Uriel) who govern all the angels who surround the Divine Throne in the Seventh Heaven.

He is the supreme archangel of the Sephirah Yesod (Foundation). He is the angel who announced the coming birth of Jesus to Mary, and revealed the Koran to Muhammad.

He is also an angel of the four terrestrial winds (or the four cardinal directions) - where he is the angel of Water and the North. (Or in some cases the West.) He is also set over sacred herbs and fruits, as the angel who "maketh the fruit ripen."

Mar 26 – *Cordad Sal* (Festival of Zoroaster's birth): Zoroaster was the founder of the Zoroastrian Religion of Persia. At the time of the birth of Jesus, it was considered the world's dominant religion – and the three Magi who visited the manger were Zoroastrian Priests. The religion had a massive impact on both Christianity and later Islam, not to mention the Solomonic Tradition. We still venerate him as the author of the *Chaldean Oracles of Zoroaster* (though it is unlikely they are Zoroastrian in origin). We also quote him as an authority when we say "Change not the barbarous names of evocation..." Plus, it is quite likely the Solomonic insistence upon the presence of fire for all consecrations is a Zoroastrian influence.

Mar 29 – Good Friday: Christian holiday commemorating the day of the Crucifixion. Always falls on the Friday before Easter – the time between the two marking the time Jesus spent in the tomb.

In the Enochian system of *Gebofal* (entering the Forty Nine Gates of Understanding) can begin on the morning after Good Friday. (Compare to the Jewish practice of "Counting the

Omer" at Passover.)

Mar 31 – Easter: Christian Holiday celebrating the resurrection of Christ. Essentially the Christian Spring Festival, marked by ancient pagan symbols of fertility such as decorated eggs and rabbits.

April 2024

Apr 1 – Veneralia (Feast of Venus): Celebrated the Goddess Venus Verticordia ("Changer of Hearts"), love, sex, and fertility. Linked to the dawning of Spring. This is a good day to honor Anael and other Venus Angels.

– Feast of St. Anael: (Hanael, Haniel) Anael is the supreme archangel of Venus and Friday, as well as the third heaven called Sagun. She is princess of the Choir Elohim. She is an angel of passion - including love, sex, beauty, and artistic inspiration - but also anger, hatred, and war. She is closely related to Goddess figures such as Aphrodite, Ishtar, and Inanna; as well as the Wiccan Goddess.

As Hanael ("Grace of God") she is an extremely exalted angel in charge of the Sephirah Netzach (Divine Victory).

Apr 19 – Feast of St. Expeditus: Died April 303 CE. A Roman centurion who was martyred in Armenia (in modern Turkey), for converting to Christianity. Famous today as the patron saint of speedy cases, and also helps one overcome procrastination. When you need something fast, ask St. Expedite. Best to work with him on Wednesdays. When he comes through, make an offering of flowers and pound cake, and thank him publically, or he may revoke his gifts.

April 22 - Passover begins: *Pesach.* Passover is an approximately week-long feast period, celebrating the liberation of the Hebrew people from Egyptian slavery. It is also a spring festival, similar in concept to the Christian celebration from Good Friday to Easter. And all of these are near the spring equinox for good reason.

      The Rite outlined in the *Book of Abramelin* to contact one's Holy Guardian Angel begins on this day. This is also the day one would begin the practice of "Counting the Omer" (or entering the Fifty Gates of Wisdom) – lasting until the Festival of Weeks (*Shavuot*).

Apr 23 – Feast of St. George: A Great Martyr and one of the most popular interceding Saints in Christian history.

Apr 30 – Walpurgisnacht: Also Witches' Night. Falls on the eve of St. Walpurga. In German folklore, it was called *Hexennacht* (Witches' Night) because it was believed a coven of witches met in the nearby mountains on this night. Bonfires were even built to fend off the witches. Being the eve of Mayday, and springtime celebration associated with sex, Walpurgisnacht eventually became a carnival-style celebration of drunken revelry.

Because of it's association with both sinful behavior and witchcraft, Walpurgisnacht has had a long association with the tales of Faust - see the Faustian grimoire tradition. This could be a perfect day for a "Feast of Faust" if you work that path.

May 2024

May 1 – Beltane (Mayday): Midpoint between spring equinox and summer solstice. Often marked by fire festivals celebrating the spring, budding crops, and the mating of both animal and humans. In modern Neopaganism, Beltane celebrates the wedding of the Lord and Lady, and the return of life after long winter.

May 15 – *Mercuralia* (Feast of Mercury): Celebrated the Roman God Mercury. This is also a good day to honor Raphael and other Angels of Mercury.

- Feast of Saint Dymphnia: Celebrates the Patron Saint of victims of child sexual abuse, incest, and rape, as well as those suferring from depression, anxiety, epilipsy, mental illness, and the possessed.

May 19 – Feast of St. Dunstan: Celebrates the Patron Saint of Metallurgists and Alchemists. The latter patronage was recognized in the court of Holy Roman Emperor Rudolph II (between 1576-1612). This was during the same period Edward Kelley sought the help of Dr. John Dee in deciphering an alchemical text he had found named *The Book of Dunstan*. There were, in fact, several alchemical texts attributed to this Sain.

May 24 – Feast of Hermes Trismegistus: "Thrice Great Hermes", the Prophet of the Hermetic Tradition, and supposed author of the *Corpus Hermeticum* and the *Emerald Tablet*. Equated with the deity Thoth-Hermes. His feast day is said to coincide with the "ancient pagan holy day of the Triple Goddess" - however (to date) I can only find reference to an annual gypsy festival in France (The Mothers of Arles) that begins on May 24.

I have seen this date listed as a Feast of the God Hermes, but so far have failed to link this date to his known festival (the *Hermaea* – which appears to have been an annual Olympics-style event held in various parts of Greece). I should also point out the Egyptian Feast of Thoth is July 19th.

May 27 – Memorial Day (USA): Commemorates fallen soldiers. Good time for work with Mars and the spirits of those who gave their lives in service.

May 30 – Feast of Corpus Christi: Celebrates the presence of the body and blood of Christ in the elements of the Eucharist.

June 2024

June 2 – Feast of St. Elmo: Celebrates the Patron Saint of sailors. Origin of the term "St. Elmo's Fire."

June 11 – Festival of Weeks begins: *Shavuot.* Commemorates the giving of the Torah at Mt. Sinai.

      This day would end the practice of "Counting the Omer" (or entering the Fifty Gates of Wisdom).

June 13 – Feast of St. Anthony: Celebrates the Patron Saint of lost persons and objects.

June 15 – Feast of St. Vitus: Celebrates the Patron Saint of actors, comedians, dancers, and dogs. Invoked against epilepsy, oversleeping, rheumatic chorea, snake bites, and storms.

June 19 – Feast of Saint Blessed Rose: Celebrates a patron Saint of healing, the poor, and orphans. Saint Margaretha Flesch, aka Maria Rosa, aka Mother Rose, now Blessed Rose, established the Franciscan Sisters of the Blessed Virgin Mary of the Angels. Even long before she became a nun, she had established herself as a nurse and especially cared for the poor and orphans. She is also the great-great-great aunt of Sandra Tabatha Cicero, co-chief of the Hermetic Order of the Golden Dawn.

June 20 – Summer Solstice (Litha): Also midsummer. Longest day of the year, shortest night – after which the days begin to grow shorter again. In modern Neopaganism, Litha celebrates the overthow of the Lord of the Waxing Sun by the Lord of the Waning Sun, so the summer heat will not overtake the world.

June 21 – Feast of St. Lazarus: Often confused with Lazarus of Bethany, who was resurrected by Jesus in the Gospel of John, this is actually Lazarus the Beggar – described in a parable called "The Rich Man and the Beggar Lazarus" told in the Gospel of Luke. He is the Patron Saint of the poor and the sick, often invoked to heal the sick. He is also associated with dogs, and some churches even offer blessings for dogs on his feast day. (Though some conflate his feast day with that of the resurrected Lazarus – December 17th.) In Afro-Caribbean Tradition, St. Lazarus is syncretized with Babalú-Ayé, who is also concerned with healing the sick.

July 2024

July 5 – Feast of Anubis: Celebrates the Egyptian God of the Tomb and embalming. Anubis is a psychopomp (guide in the underworld), and later appears in the *Greek Magical Papyri* as an intermediary spirit. Connections to Cerberus.

July 13 – Festival of Re: (Or Ra.) Celebrates the Egyptian Sun God. Husband of Nut, creator of the world.

July 13 – Birth of John Dee: Dr. John Dee (b. July 13, 1587), counselor and astrologer to Queen Elizabeth I, was an important figure in Elizabethan England and its movement toward eventual Empire. He also recorded the system of Enochian Magick skryed by Edward Kelley.

July 16 – Festival of Set: Celebrates the birthday of Set, God of the desert and warfare, brother and murderer of Osiris. Husband of Nephthys. One of the nine principal Egyptian Deities (the *Ennead*).

July 18 – Festival of Nephthys: Celebrates the birthday of Nephthys, sister of Isis, and wife of Set. She was often invoked for protection, and was called "the useful Goddess." One of the nine principal Egyptian Deities (the *Ennead*).

July 19 – Feast of Thoth: Celebrates the Egyptian God of wisdom, language, writing, and magick. Thoth has close relationships with the later Gnostic concept of the Logos.

July 20 – Feast of St. Margaret the Virgin: Celebrates the Patron Saint of childbirth, pregnant women, dying people, peasants, exiles, and the falsely accused.

July 25 – Feast of St. Christopher: Celebrates the Patron Saint of Travelers.

July 26 – Feast of Enoch: Biblical forefather, seventh generation from Adam, grandfather of Noah. Legend depicts him traveling into the heavens in the company of angels to explore the seven heavenly realms, gaining access to the celestial Book of Life, and returning to Earth to pen 366 books of wisdom based on what he learned there. John Dee was told by his angelic contacts that Enoch's wisdom has been lost, but would be returned to humanity through him (Dee) and Kelley in the form of the Enochian system of angel magick.

July 27 – Feast of St. Pataleon: Celebrates the Patron Saint of physicians, midwives, livestock, and the lottery. Invoked against headaches, consumption, locusts, witchcraft, accidents and loneliness. Comes to the aid of crying children

August 2024

Aug 1 – Lughnasadh (Lammas): A harvest festival. In modern Neopagaism, Lammas commemorates both the fallen Solar God (see summer solstice) and the sacrifice of the Grain God via harvesting. (Reference *John Barleycorn*.)

- Edward Kelley born: Edward Kelley (August 1, 1555 – November 1, 1597) was an English occultist and alchemist. He is most famous as the skryer employed by Dr. John Dee in the reception of the Enochian system of angel magick. However he also had a career as an alchemist in Emperor Rudolph's court in Prague.

Aug 13 – Feast of Hekate (Hekatesia): Celebrates the Queen of the Underworld and Night, the (triple) Crossroads, and of the Three Realms (Celestial, Earthy, and Chthonic). In the medieval era, She became associated with Selene (as her celestial aspect), Artemis (earthly aspect), and Persephone (chthonic aspect), and was believed to have power over all three realms and the natural spirits who reside in them. Modern pagans invoke her as the Triple Goddess who governs nature, and protects children and mothers.

September 2024

Sep 2 – Feast of Osiris: Celebrates the Egyptian Lord of Grain and the Underworld. Later became a Solar Deity. Egyptian mythos credits him as the founder of civilization and the first Pharaoh. One of the nine principal Egyptian Deities (the *Ennead*).

Sep 13 – *Epulum Jovis* (Feast of Jupiter): Celebrated the Roman God Jupiter. This is a good day to honor Sachiel and other Jupiter Angels.

Sep 15 Agrippa born: Heinrich Cornelius Agrippa von Nettesheim (September 14, 1486 – February 18, 1535) was a famous author, scholar, physician, and occultist. He is most famous for his *Three Books of Occult Philosophy*, a primary (if later) source-book for the Solomonic tradition.

Sep 17 – Feast of St. Sophia the Martyr: Died 137 CE. Sophia (Wisdom) is the Mother Goddess of the Gnostics – equated with Mother Mary, the Queen of Heaven, the Shekhina, Aima Elohim, and the Soul of the World. She gave birth to the Demiurgos (Creator) as well as innumerable angels.

Sophia the Martyr is not officially equated with Her,

however her story suggests she may in fact be a metaphor for the Goddess. As it is told, Sophia had three daughters: Hope, Faith, and Charity. These daughters were taken from her, tortured, and murdered in an effort to force Sophia to renounce her faith. She held fast, buried her daughters, and remained by their graves until she also died three days later. This sounds very much like a metaphorical tale of mankind's disdain for Mother Sophia (Wisdom) and the gifts She brings to humanity.

- Feast of Hathor: Celebrates the Egyptian Solar Goddess of passion, beauty, love, and motherhood. She was also a fierce protector, perhaps most famous for her murderous rampage against humanity when she learned some of them were plotting against Re.

Sep 20 – Feast of St. Eustace: Celebrates the Patron Saint of fire prevention, firefighters, trappers, hunters, hunting, and torture victims. He is invoked against fire and in difficult situations.

Sep 22 – Autumnal Equinox (Mabon): At this time the day and night are the same length, each being exactly twelve clock-hours long. Mabon is a harvest and in-gathering festival (preparation for the coming winter). In modern Neopaganism, Mabon celebrates the funeral of the fallen Sun God (see summer solstice and Lughnasadh), and is a time of thanksgiving.

Sep 24 – Paracelsus passes: Paracelsus (1493/4 – September 24, 1541), was born Theophrastus von Hohenheim. He was a physician, astrologer, and alchemist. His writings established the Elementals (Salamadar, Undine, Sylph, and Gnome) in Western occultism, and his alchemical influence was widespread. (See Kathy McDonald's *Pauline Arts Adventure*.)

Sep 26 – Feasts of St. Cyprian and St Justina (of Antioch): (Died 304 CE) Said to be a Bishop of Antioch, but no records exist of a Bishop Cyprian there. Legends says before his conversion he was a powerful Pagan sorcerer. He sent demons against St Justina, but she easily defeated them with the sign of the Cross. Impressed with this power, Cyprian made the sign of the Cross upon himself and thus freed himself from demonic influence. While some accounts insist he renounced all magick, others suggest he continued to practice the occult arts alongside his Christian faith.   He is famous today as the Patron Saint of Sorcerers and Necromancers. See The *Grimoire of St. Cyprian: Clavis Inferni* for an example of a Cyprianic Grimoire.

Both are said to have been Martyred in 304 CE during the persecutions of the Roman Emperor Diocletian in Nicomedia.

Sep 29 – Michaelmas: St. Michael is the Archangel of the Sun and Sunday – the representative of God's Light here on Earth. His name means "Who is Like God", and he is prince of the Choir of Melelkhim. He is the highest archangel (besides Metatron himself) and sits at the right-hand of the Divine Throne. He is also the angel of the fourth heaven called Machen.

As the Angel of the Sun, he is the General of the Heavenly Armies, the High Priest of the Celestial Temple, Patron of Israel and the quintessential Guardian Angel. He is patron to soldiers (especially para-troopers and pilots), police officers and warriors of all types.

Some traditions also consider him an Angel of Mercury, and the supreme archangel of the Sephirah Hod (Brilliance). In his Mercurial aspect, he judges the dead with his scales and guides the souls to Paradise or Gehenna according to their deeds in life. He is a benevolent Angel of Death, and carries the souls of the righteous to heaven. As an archangel with chthonic associations, he is an angel of war and plague as well as of protection and healing. In some traditions, Michael is considered a divine physician and healer on par with Raphael. He is patron of EMTs, emergency workers and all first responders.

He is also an angel of the four terrestrial winds (or the four cardinal directions) - where he is the angel of Fire and the East.

(Or in some cases the South.) He is also one of the Four (along with Gabriel, Raphael, and Uriel) who govern all the angels who surround the Divine Throne in the Seventh Heaven.

    - Feast of Archangels: Michael feast day (Michaelmas) is also called the Feast of the Archangels – primarily of the four ruling Archangels, but also of all angels in general. Therefore, any Archangel can be honored on this day, either singly or in groups. (If in groups, the Four ruling Archangels are traditionally honored together. All seven Planetary Angels could also be honored together.)

October 2024

Oct 2 – Feast of the Holy Guardian Angels: Also called the "Memorial of the Holy Guardian Angels." Celebrates Guardian Angels.

Oct 4 – Feast of St. Francis: Celebrates the Patron Saint of Wild Animals.

Oct 7 – Feast of Maat: Celebrates the Egyptian Goddess of truth, judgment, law, and morality. Maat presides over the scales that weigh one's heart in the underworld judgment chamber. She also directs the motions of the stars and the affairs of mortal lives – making her an Egyptian forerunner of the Fates, and a Goddess of astrology.

Oct 9 – Reginald Scot (Scott) passes: Reginald Scot (d. October 9, 1599) is most famous as the author of *The Discoverie of Witchcraft*, published in 1584. While it was written to expose witchcraft as a hoax (revealing many of the techniques conjurors used to impress their clients), it went on to preserve and even popularize many aspects of classical magick.

Oct 16 – Feast of Tabernacles begins: *Sukkot.* A week-long feast period celebrating the Exodus, and commemorating the end of the harvest season and in-gathering of the final crops. Note its proximity to the autumnal equinox.

The final seven days of the Rite outlined in the *Book of Abramelin* to contact one's Holy Guardian Angel begins on this day.

Oct 17 – Feast of Sekhmet: Celebrates the Egyptian Lion-Goddess. A fierce Solar Warrior Goddess, as well as a healer. She has close relationships to both Bast and Hathor.

Oct 24 – Feast of St. Raphael: St. Raphael is an angel of Mercury and Wednesday, as well as the second heaven called Raquie. His name means "Healer of God", and his is prince of the Choir of Beni Elohim. He is one of the Four (along with Gabriel, Michael, and Uriel) who govern all the angels who surround the Divine Throne in the Seventh Heaven. He is the angel of healing and medicine.

He is also a psychopomp, guiding souls in the underworld - likely related to this is his function as an angel of healing. He is also the angel of science and knowledge.

In some traditions he is an angel of the Sun, where he is the supreme archangel of the Sephirah Tiphareth (Beauty/Majesty).

He is also an angel of the four terrestrial winds (or the four cardinal directions) - where he is the angel of Air and the West. (Or in some cases the East.)

Oct 28 – Feast of St. Jude: Celebrates the Patron Saint of lost causes (especially in severe health issues and life/death situations) and of the impossible.

Oct 31 – Halloween (Samhain): Also All Hallow's Eve. Midpoint between autumnal equinox and summer solstice. Samhain is a celebration of ancestors and others who have passed on – a "Day of the Dead" style festival. (Secular Halloween lost contact with those roots for a while, but is slowly rediscovering them.) In modern Neopaganism, it marks the new year and celebrates the entrance of the fallen Solar God (see summer solstice) into the underworld. The veils between the physical and spiritual worlds are thin at this time, making it a good time for evocation and divination.

- Feast of Bast: Celebrates the Egyptian Goddess of Cats. Associated with perfumes, and known to be a fierce protector of the home and children. Has a close relationship with the Lion-Goddess Sekhmet.

November 2024

Nov 1 – Feast of All Saints (All Saints Day): Celebrates all Saints, both known and unknown.

– Feast of Santa Muerte: Celebrates Lady Death.

Nov 3 – Feast of Saint Martin de Porres: Celebrates the Patron Saint of Peru, domestic animals, veterinarians, health workers, innkeepers, and race relations.

Nov 8 – Feast of St. Uriel (Auriel): St. Uriel has never been definitively placed as the prince of any specific angelic Choir. However, he is one of the Four (along with Gabriel, Raphael, and Michael) who govern all the angels who surround the Divine Throne in the Seventh Heaven. His name means "Light of God."

He is also an angel of the four terrestrial winds (or the four cardinal directions) - where he is the angel of Earth and the South. (Or in some cases the North.) In the Book of Enoch, Uriel is the angel who directs the motions of the stars and planets.

While we generally consider Uriel an angel of the Earth Element, he is in some cases associated with the Sun (and Sunday) - since his name means "Light of God." In some traditions he is an angel of poetry and writing, and carries a scroll representing wisdom.

Yet, he is known as a dark and even dangerous angel of both vengeance and repentance, who "watches over thunder and terror" and shows little pity to wrongdoers. He is said to preside over Tartarus – thereby associating him directly with the underworld.

But he is also an angel of salvation. Some legends even place him as the guardian of the Gate of Eden, with the famous Flaming Sword in his hand. He is the embodiment of the mystical phrase "The Light which shineth in darkness, yet the darkness comprehendeth it not."

In the Solomonic system, Uriel often appears as an angel of divination and a gate-keeper. That makes him particularly suited as an angel of revelation, a revealer of secrets, and an angel of divination. It also makes Uriel an intermediary spirit who can bring other angels and spirits to the magick circle.

Uriel was never given his own feast day, instead sharing a day with the other three ruling Archangels on November 8: The Synaxis of the Archangel Michael and the Other Bodiless Powers.

Nov 11 – Feast of St. Martin of Tours: Also known as San Martin Caballero (Saint Martin of Horses). Patron Saint of those who must depend on strangers' kindness (including shopkeepers and travelers), as well as truck drivers, and gamblers.

Nov 15 – Feast of St. Albert the Great (Albertus Magnus):
Albertus Magnus (d. November 15, 1280) was a Dominican friar and Bishop. He had an interest in astrology and natural philosophy, which likely led to later legends of his being a magician and alchemist. He has since been cannonized as a saint, patron of medical technicians, natural sciences, philosophers, scientists, and students.

  - Feast of the Ennead in the House of Ra: A feast-day dedicated to all nine principle Gods of Egypt: Geb, Nut, Tefnut, Shu, Osiris, Isis, Horus, Set, and Nephthys.

Nov 25 – Feast of Moses: The Biblical prophet who led the Exodus of the Hebrew people from Egyptian slavery, led them through the years or wandering, and penned the five books of the Torah. He is also purported to be the author of the famous grimoire *The Sixth and Seventh Books of Moses*.

  – Feast of St. Catherine of Alexandria: St. Catherine is one of the Great Martyrs, and during the Middle Ages was an extremely popular intercessor on par with the Virgin Mary. (The legend of her martyrdom may have been adapted from the record of the murder of the Greek philosopher Hypatia.)

Nov 28 – Thanksgiving: American day of thanksgiving for family, friends, and a good harvest (abundance). It takes place on the 4th Thursday of November (both 4 and Thursday are sacred to Jupiter) when the Sun resides in Sagittarius (ruled by Jupiter). It's primary symbol is the Cornucopia and it celebrates abundance. Altogether this makes Thanksgiving a very Jupiterian holiday.

– Feast of Sachiel (Zadkiel): Sachiel is the supreme archangel of Jupiter and Thursday, as well as the sixth heaven called Zebul. He is the angel of righteousness, benevolence, mercy, forgiveness and freedom. His name in Hebrew is Zadkiel ("Righteous of God"). He is prince of the Choir Chashmalim (Brilliant Ones).

As Zadkiel, he is an extremely exalted angel in charge of the Sephirah Chesed (Divine Mercy). Zadkiel and Iophiel (the Intelligence of the planet Jupiter) are both considered standard-bearers who follow Michael into battle.

December 2024

Dec 4 – Feast of St. Barbara: Celebrates the Patron Saint of those who work with explosives, firefighters, prisoners, soldiers, and mathematicians. She is also invoked against lightning or sudden and violent death. Patron Saint of Santa Barbara, CA.

Dec 6 – Feast of St. Nicholas: Also known as Saint Nicholas Day. Celebrates the Patron Saint of children, the falsely accused, repentant thieves, brewers, coopers, sailors, fishermen, merchants, and pharmacists (to name just a few!). He is, of course, the same St. Nick also known as Santa Claus.

Dec 17 – Feast of Solomon, Righteous Prophet and King: In the Eastern Orthodox Church, Solomon is commemorated as a saint. His feast day is celebrated on the Sunday of the Holy Forefathers, two Sundays before the Great Feast of the Nativity of the Lord (Dec 25th). Famous for his wisdom and his power to control both animals and spirits at will, he is supposed to be the author of several famous grimoires named the *Key of Solomon* or some variant thereof.

  – Saturnalia (Feast of Saturn): Celebrated the founding of the Temple of Saturn in Rome. Takes place near the entrance of the Sun into Capricorn, which is ruled by Saturn. This is a good day to honor Cassiel and other Saturn Angels.

– Feast of St. Cassiel: (Zaphkiel, Tzaphkiel, Qaphziel, Kafziel)

Cassiel is the archangel of the planet Saturn and Saturday, and of the seventh heaven called Araboth. Prince of the Choir of Aralim. He is the Angel of tears and solitude, of repentance, of inheritance, and of limitations.

As Zaphkiel ("Knowledge of God"), he is an exalted angel in charge of the Sephirah Binah (Divine Understanding). His relationship to Saturn likely makes him an angel of agriculture and the earth, of wealth, as well giving him associations with the dead and the underworld.

As Kafziel, he governs the death of kings, and (along with Hizkiel) is a chief aid to Gabriel when that angel bears his standard into battle.

Dec 21 – Winter Solistice (Yule): Also Midwinter and Christmastide. Shortest day of the year, longest night. Yule in modern Neopaganism celebrates the birth of the Sun, after which the days begin to grow longer again. Has obvious connections to the Solar Feasts of December 25th.

- Feast of Isis: Celebrates the wife of Osiris and the Mother Goddess of Egypt. She is one of the nine principal Egyptian Deities (the *Ennead*).

Dec 25 – *Dies Natalis Solis Invicti* (Feast of Sol): The name of this feast means "Birthday of the Unconquered Sun." Held near the winter solstice, but timed to take place *after* the days of Saturnalia. (Likely the origin of Dec 25th as the accepted birthday of Christ.) This is the first of the Twelve Days of Christmas, which end on January 5th (directly followed by Epiphany). It is also a good day to honor Michael and other Solar Angels.

– Christmas: The feast of the birthday of Jesus. See the above notes for *Dies Natalis Solis Invicti* (the Feast of Sol).

Dec 25 – *Hanukkah* begins: The Festival of Lights, lasting for eight nights. Commemorates the re-dedication of the second Temple at the time of the Maccabean Revolt. Tradition holds the Maccabees only had enough oil for the sacred lamps to burn for one night, but it miraculously lasted for eight nights. There are likely connections to older Palestinian pagan "festivals of light" (see the winter solstice).

For more great books on the Western Mysteries,

classes, traditional magical tools and supplies,

Visit us at

Doc Solomon's Occult Curios

http://docsolomons.com

For News, Updates, Photos, Videos, Discounts, and More

Join our Facebook family

https://www.facebook.com/DocSolomons/

And check us out on YouTube

https://www.youtube.com/c/docsolomons

Printed in Great Britain
by Amazon